# Your Life in Poems

**Edited by Charles Doersch**

## SCHOLASTIC INC.

New York   Toronto   London   Auckland   Sydney
Mexico City   New Delhi   Hong Kong   Buenos Aires

## Cover Illustrations

tl: Melissa Leslie, *Nicole*/Artwork from The Scholastic Art & Writing Awards/www.artandwriting.org via SODA; tr: Vantino Peaches, *Self Portrait*/Artwork from The Scholastic Art & Writing Awards/www.artandwriting.org via SODA; bl: Hasan Marius, *Untitled*/Artwork from The Scholastic Art & Writing Awards/www.artandwriting.org via SODA; br: Anne Lindberg, *Self*/Artwork from The Scholastic Art and Writing Awards/www.artandwriting.org via SODA

Acknowledgments appear on page 40, which constitutes an extension of this copyright page.

Developed by ONO Books in cooperation with Scholastic Inc.

Compilation copyright © 2003 by Scholastic Inc.
All rights reserved. Published by Scholastic Inc.
Printed in the U.S.A.

ISBN 0-439-59813-3

3   4   5   6   7   8   9   10      23      12 11 10 09 08 07

# Contents

# Welcome to This Book

*What kind of people do you think write poems? Old people who can't even remember what it's like to be young? Boring people who have no life? Bookworms who live in libraries?*

Think again. These days poets are rap artists, adventurers, athletes, and students. They all choose to write poetry because they have something to say. They know that poetry is a powerful way to say it.

So what matters to you about yourself, love, family, and school? Read these poems. You might be surprised to find your life reflected there.

**Target Words** Here are some words that will help you understand the poems in this book.

- **emotion:** a strong feeling such as happiness, love, anger, or grief
  *Writing poetry is one way to express an emotion.*

- **repetition:** doing or saying something over and over again
  *Repetition can draw attention to ideas or sounds.*

- **rhythm:** a regular beat
  *The rhythm of a poem is its music.*

**Reader Tips** Here's how to get the most from these poems.

- **Chapter Titles** Chapter titles express the main idea of the poems in each chapter. The first chapter, "In the Mirror," includes poems about personal identity. Use the chapter titles to get a better idea of what each poem is about.

- **Theme** The theme is the overall message or idea about life. To find the theme, notice the results of the narrator's words or actions. Then think about any lesson that the narrator may have learned in the process.

# 1

# In the Mirror

### Take a look at yourself.

What do you see when you look in the mirror? The obvious things are right in front of you. You can see your hair, your face, and your clothes. But what happens when you look deeper?

Is that your father's nose? Are those your mother's eyes? What does your face say about your **heritage**? And what does that have to do with who you really are?

How do you look today? What does your style say about how you are? Are you dressing to impress? If so, whom do you hope will notice? What do you want them to think?

As you read these poems, imagine yourself in them. What do you see?

**As you read these poems, imagine yourself in them.**

# Mutt

When you see me
    Do you see
The color of Africa?
Do you see the rhythm of Cuba?
    Do you see
The strength of the Cherokee?
    Do you see
The **empire** of China?
    Do you see
The **tropics** of the Caribbean?
If not, look closer.

*Zarinah James*

## Heads Up!

*How do most people use the word* mutt*? Do they use it in a positive way or a negative way? How do you think the poet is using the word here as the title?*

# Maybe

if I stretch myself tall
as a tree, if I sway
and pull my stomach in
until it touches my spine
and curl my hair into a river
of light, if I borrow
my sister's dress that whispers
when I glide without touching
the floor, and if I try a laugh
that ripples green with mystery
maybe he'll forget it's just me
hiding inside.

*Pat Mora*

## Heads Up!

**What occasion do you think the narrator of this poem is getting ready for? What do you think she wants to happen?**

# The Man Hands I Wear

The man hands I wear are shy because
they hide behind my back.
They're big and out of proportion;
they don't feel like my own.

As I walk, my hands pull me forward
and people stare.
They become shy again
and hide behind my back.

Later, they come out again
and I spin around,
the weight of my hands pulling me
this way and that.
Those evil hands,
so big and ugly.

I sit on the stoop on my brownstone,
stuffing those big hands under my thighs,
rocking on them.

I take them out to cover
my wet, teary face and suddenly
they're the best.
They're perfect.
I pat down my fluffy hair
and feel the air rush past
my perfect fingers.
I hold them out for all to see.

*See, see.*
Hold, hold these perfect hands
and tell me they're not the best,
the softest, and
my own.

*Lia-taré Brown*

## Heads Up!

*How does the narrator feel about her hands at the beginning of the poem? How does she feel about them at the end? What do you think caused the change?*

# Learning English

Life
to understand me
you have to know Spanish
feel it in the blood of your soul.

If I speak another language
and use different words
for feelings that will always stay the same
I don't know
if I'll continue being
the same person.

*Luis Alberto Ambroggio*
*translated by Lori M. Carlson*

## Heads Up!

**Would you be the same person in any language? Think about it.**

# 2

# The Heart Sings

**What kinds of songs does your heart sing?**

If you've ever been in love, you know the feeling is almost impossible to put into words. Still, you probably want to tell everyone in sight how you feel.

But how do you feel? Love has more ups and downs than a giant roller coaster. One minute you're thinking, "Has the sky always been such a pretty shade of blue?" The next minute, you feel like you have your own personal storm cloud following you around.

These poets have been there, too. And they have put these strong **emotions** into words. Do they sound familiar to you?

Love is often filled with ups and downs.

# Maurice

You stumbled into my life
    without **grace**
    or **charm;**
    without wealth
    or experience;
    without hope
    or even luck.
But when you wavered,
    you slipped
    you tripped
and grabbed my hand
I laughed
and fell
        in love
with you.

*Maria Galati*

## Heads Up!

*Look up the words* charm *and* grace *in the glossary. Why is it surprising that Maurice is without these qualities?*

## Love Letter

it has snowed
on this page
and there are tracks
as of a small
animal lost
in the white weather

in the cold battle
of breath
yours forms
the only cloud
on which I can rest
my head

*Linda Pastan*

## Heads Up!

**What do you think the tracks of a small animal lost in white weather really are? Here's a hint. Think of the tracks as dark marks on a white background.**

# Craig

if I were to see you from a block away
i'd know you by your walk
i'd know it's you by your smile,
strains of dark black straight hair, and
baggy and sagging jeans with your
gangster lean
if i felt hands on my head
i'd know those were your hands
big, but with a gentle touch
with the smell of fresh cologne
if i heard a voice coming from a whisper
i'd know that they were your words
by the way they flow inside and out
like the sounds coming from
playing my alto sax

*Jaclyn M. Smith*

**─Heads Up!─**
*How well does the narrator know Craig?*
*How can you tell? What information does*
*the narrator give?*

# 3

# It's All Relative

### *What gives you that family feeling?*

How many times have your parents told you to pick your socks up off the floor? to feed the cat? to get off the phone? Parents are masters of **repetition.** And the more they repeat these things, the more you tune them out. Maybe they should try writing a poem.

In poetry, repetition has the opposite effect. Repeating a word or a phrase can help fix a sound or idea in your mind.

And talk about repetition. Family members are the people you see every day. You know them really well. That's why the feelings you have about them run deep.

Here are four poems about family. These poems are about different ways of being together and apart. Can you relate?

**Can you relate to these poems about family?**

# The Only One

Vicky has six brothers
and their house vibrates in the evening
with radio sounds
and yelling from floor
to
floor.
I sit on the stairs
and drink the house in
between dinner with tons
of food and so much talk and
laughter it almost becomes
one loud food-filled yell.
And it isn't like home
where sometimes (if everybody is working late)
I'm the only one
eating at our kitchen table,
and only the sound of the ceiling fan
spins against the quiet.

*Angela Johnson*

## Beach Muscles

My big brother is pumping iron,
doing curls and sweaty squats
in a corner of the garage.

But when Mom asks his help
to lift some rugs in the basement,
he moans: *Whoa! That's heavy!*

and that makes Mom laugh.
*What are these for?* she asks,
grabbing his **biceps.**

*These aren't for work,* he says.
*These are beach muscles;
you know, just for show.*

*Ralph Fletcher*

**—Heads Up!—**
*What's the tone of this poem? Serious?
Funny? Angry? What words give you a clue?*

# Forgotten

Mom came home one day
and said my father had died.
Her eyes all red.
Crying for some stranger.
Couldn't think of anything to do,
so I walked around Beaver
telling the kids
and feeling important.
Nobody else's dad had died.
But then
nobody else's dad had worn
red-striped pajamas
and nobody else's dad had made
stuffed animals talk
and nobody else's dad had gone away
nine years ago.

Nobody else's dad had been so loved by
    a four-year-old.
And so forgotten by one
now
thirteen.

*Cynthia Rylant*

**—Heads Up!—**

*The phrase "nobody else's dad" comes up five times in this poem. How does this help you understand how the narrator feels?*

## I never saw the road . . .

I never saw the road between our
house and Grandma's.
By the time we hit the highway,
I'd be curled up, asleep on the back seat.
Mom would shake my arm to wake me
as our old station wagon pulled into the
**makeshift** dirt driveway.
Grandma's house was a mansion to me
through my groggy, half-opened eyes,
with stone porch steps
painted green,
hiding between the gardenia bushes.
Inside, the house was like a
Chinese herb shop,
dried shrimp smells dangling
between the ginseng tea and
sugared fruit.
Grandma used to give me pieces of
candy wrapped in rice paper that I called
Handi-wrap.

I'd suck on the jellied sweetness
until the wrapper melted away
just like the trees and telephone poles
between our house and Grandma's.
I sometimes think that if I
doze off in the car today,
I'll wake up in the old station wagon
almost there.

*Donna Lee*

## Heads Up!

*The wrapper on the candy "melted away"*
*just like the trees and telephone poles.*
*What else has melted away in this poem?*

# School Days

### *What's it like on your side of the desk?*

Why write a poem about school? You spend all day there. Isn't that enough?

Well, think about it. What happens in school? You sweat out exams, you make friends and lose them, and if you're lucky, you gain a little knowledge along the way. What better material could there be for poetry?

The three poems that follow are all about school and learning. As you read, pay attention to their **rhythm.** Need an example? Go to a school game. "We're tough. We're rough. And now our team has had enough." That's rhythm.

Don't worry. These poems aren't cheers for school. But they do talk about what it's like to be on your side of the desk.

What would you add?

**Not all learning takes place in the classroom. What have you learned from life?**

# The History Teacher

Trying to protect his students' innocence
he told them the Ice Age was really just
the Chilly Age, a period of a million years
when everyone had to wear sweaters.

And the Stone Age became the Gravel Age,
named after the long driveways of the time.

The **Spanish Inquisition** was nothing more
than an outbreak of questions such as
"How far is it from here to Madrid?"
"What do you call the **matador's** hat?"

The **War of the Roses** took place in a garden
and the **Enola Gay** dropped one tiny atom
on Japan.

The children would leave his classroom
for the playground to **torment** the weak
and the smart,
mussing up their hair and breaking their glasses,

while he gathered up his notes and walked home
past flower beds and white picket fences,
wondering if they would believe that soldiers
in the **Boer War** told long, rambling stories
designed to make the enemy nod off.

*Billy Collins*

## Heads Up!

*The teacher in this poem is trying to protect his students. What do you think he's trying to protect them from? Do you think he should? Why or why not?*

## Numbers

I like the generosity of numbers.
The way, for example,
they are willing to count
anything or anyone:
two pickles, one door to the room,
eight dancers dressed as swans.

I like the **domesticity** of addition—
add two cups of milk and stir—
the sense of plenty: six plums
on the ground, three more
falling from the tree.

And multiplication's school
of fish times fish,
whose silver bodies breed
beneath the shadow
of a boat.

Even subtraction is never loss,
just addition somewhere else:
five sparrows take away two,

the two in someone else's
garden now.

There's an **amplitude** to long division,
as it opens Chinese take-out
box by paper box,
inside every folded cookie
a new fortune.

And I never fail to be surprised
by the gift of an odd remainder,
footloose at the end:
forty-seven divided by eleven equals four,
with three remaining.

Three boys beyond their mothers' call,
two Italians off to the sea,
one sock that isn't anywhere you look.

*Mary Cornish*

## The Unwritten

Inside this pencil
crouch words that have never been written
never been spoken
never been thought

they're hiding

they're awake in there
dark in the dark
hearing us
but they won't come out
not for love not for time not for fire

even when the dark has worn away
they'll still be there
hiding in the air
**multitudes** in days to come may walk
    through them
breathe them
be none the wiser

what script can it be
that they won't unroll
in what language
would I recognize it
would I be able to follow it
to make out the real names
of everything

maybe there aren't
many
it could be that there's only one word
and it's all we need
it's here in this pencil

every pencil in the world
is like this

*W. S. Merwin*

**Heads Up!**

***If there were only one word in your pencil,
what might that word be?***

# Write Now!

You may not have realized it, but some of the poems in this book were written by teens. So there's no reason why you can't do it, too. Not sure where to start? Try these ideas on for size.

1. **Cut Away:** Describe something that happened in your life that you have really intense feelings about.

   **Step 1:** Write it out so it fits on one page. Don't think about grammar or spelling. Just get it all out, like you were telling a friend.

   **Step 2:** Go through and circle the words that are strongest, brightest, darkest, sharpest.

   **Step 3:** Cut all the rest of the words out.

   **Step 4:** Count the number of words left. That's how many lines your poem is going to have.

   **Step 5:** Use one of the words you circled in each line.

2. **Uncommon Sense:** Build a six-line poem using all your senses.

**Line 1:** Think of an event or memory that made you feel a certain emotion. Write what you saw. (Example: the day I got a puppy)

**Line 2:** Describe a flavor that reminds you of this emotion. (Example: pink cotton candy)

**Line 3:** Pick a color and an object that together create the emotion. (Example: a rainbow-colored puddle)

**Line 4:** Imagine a **physical** feeling you've had that also reminds you of this emotion. Describe it. (Example: going uphill on a really big roller coaster)

**Line 5:** Describe the sound of something that gives you this feeling. (Example: hearing my favorite song on the radio)

**Line 6:** Start with the phrase "That's how I knew . . ." and see what you end up saying.

3. **Haiku:** Here's a beautiful Japanese type of poem. It's only three lines. But there are strict rules. There must be five syllables in the first line, seven in the second, and five in the third.

Ready? First describe an image from nature in lines one and two. Then talk about a related feeling in line three. Here's an example:

*Snow falling all day,*
*A tree sagging to the ground.*
*Still the phone won't ring.*

Think about how a sagging tree is like someone who is disappointed about not getting an expected phone call.

4. **Ad It Up:** Think of a saying or catchy slogan used in a TV commercial, like "Just do it" or "Is it in you?" Use the slogan as the **refrain** in your poem.

Ready? Write about three situations completely unrelated to the ad. End each one with the slogan from the commercial. By the time the poem is finished, the phrase will mean something very new and different.

5. **Cut and Paste:** Still in need of **inspiration**? Then start with someone else's poem.

**Step 1:** Take a poem you really like and photocopy it. How old are you? That's how many lines your new poem will have.

**Step 2:** Now take a pair of scissors and cut the copied poem up into separate words. Lay the words face down on a table so you can't see what they are.

**Step 3:** Pick out a few words at random. Use them to start a line of your new poem. Put the words together in interesting new ways. Feel free to add your own words, too.

**Step 4:** Repeat as many times as necessary!

\*     \*     \*

Remember, these ideas are supposed to be fun. So play around with them. Change the rules or make up new ones. That's the great thing about poetry. There are no rules. You can do whatever you want. Hey, how often do you get an offer like that?

# Glossary

**amplitude** *(noun)* a large or full measure; abundance (p. 31)

**bicep** *(noun)* a muscle in your upper arm (p. 21)

**Boer War** *(noun)* a war between England and Dutch residents of South Africa from 1899 to 1902 (p. 29)

**charm** *(noun)* behavior that attracts others (p. 15)

**domesticity** *(noun)* the state of having to do with the home (p. 30)

**emotion** *(noun)* a strong feeling such as happiness, love, anger, or grief (p. 13)

**empire** *(noun)* a group of countries that are under one ruler (p. 8)

**Enola Gay** *(noun)* the name of the plane that dropped an atom bomb on Japan at the end of World War II (p. 28)

**grace** *(noun)* someone who has grace acts and moves with comfort and ease (p. 15)

**heritage** *(noun)* your family background (p. 6)

**inspiration** *(noun)* anything that gets you excited to do something, usually creative (p. 37)

**makeshift** *(adjective)* put together quickly with whatever is available at the time (p. 24)

**matador** *(noun)* bullfighter (p. 28)

**multitude** *(noun)* a huge crowd of people (p. 32)

**mutt** *(noun)* a mixed-breed dog (p. 8)

**physical** *(adjective)* relating to the body (p. 35)

**refrain** *(noun)* a phrase that repeats in a poem or a song (p. 36)

**repetition** *(noun)* doing or saying something over and over again (p. 18)

**rhythm** *(noun)* a regular beat (p. 26)

**Spanish Inquisition** *(noun)* the court used by the Catholic Church in the Middle Ages to make sure people followed Church rules (p. 28)

**torment** *(noun)* to annoy someone or cause them pain on purpose (p. 28)

**tropics** *(noun)* hot areas of the earth near the equator (p. 8)

**War of the Roses** *(noun)* a civil war in England in the 1400s (p. 28)

# Acknowledgments

Grateful acknowledgment is made to the following sources for permission to reprint from previously published material. The publisher has made diligent efforts to trace the ownership of all copyrighted material in this volume and believes that all necessary permissions have been secured. If any errors or omissions have inadvertently been made, proper corrections will gladly be made in future editions.

"Mutt" by Zarinah James from QUIET STORM: VOICES OF YOUNG BLACK POETS, edited by Lydia Omolola Okutoro. Copyright © 1999 by Zarinah James. Reprinted by permission of Hyperion Books for Children, an imprint of Disney Children's Book Group, LLC.

"Maybe" from MY OWN TRUE NAME by Pat Mora. Text copyright © 2000 by Pat Mora. Reprinted by permission of Piñata Books, an imprint of Arte Público Press.

"The Man Hands I Wear" by Lia-taré Brown from MOVIN': TEEN POETS TAKE VOICE, edited by Dave Johnson. Copyright © 2000 by The New York Public Library, Astor, Lenox, and Tilden Foundations. Reprinted by permission of Orchard Books, Scholastic Inc. All rights reserved.

"Learning English" by Luis Alberto Ambroggio, translated by Lori M. Carlson. Originally published in Spanish as "Comunión." Copyright © by Luis Alberto Ambroggio. Translation copyright © 1994 by Lori M. Carlson. Reprinted by permission of Henry Holt & Co., LLC.

"Maurice" by Maria Galati from QUIET STORM: VOICES OF YOUNG BLACK POETS, edited by Lydia Omolola Okutoro. Copyright © 1999 by Maria Galati. Reprinted by permission of Hyperion Books for Children, an imprint of Disney Children's Book Group, LLC.

"Love Letter" from THE FIVE STAGES OF GRIEF by Linda Pastan. Copyright © 1978 by Linda Pastan. Reprinted by permission of W. W. Norton & Company, Inc. All rights reserved.

"Craig" by Jaclyn M. Smith from QUIET STORM: VOICES OF YOUNG BLACK POETS, edited by Lydia Omolola Okutoro. Copyright © 1999 by Jaclyn M. Smith. Reprinted by permission of Hyperion Books for Children, an imprint of Disney Children's Book Group, LLC.

"The Only One" from RUNNING BACK TO LUDIE by Angela Johnson. Text copyright © 2001 by Angela Johnson. Reprinted by permission of Orchard Books, Scholastic Inc. All rights reserved.

"Beach Muscles" from RELATIVELY SPEAKING: POEMS ABOUT FAMILY by Ralph Fletcher. Text copyright © 1999 by Ralph Fletcher. Reprinted by permission of Orchard Books, Scholastic Inc. All rights reserved.

"Forgotten" from WAITING TO WALTZ by Cynthia Rylant. Copyright © 1984 by Cynthia Rylant. Reprinted by permission of Simon & Schuster Books for Young Readers, an imprint of Simon & Schuster Children's Publishing Division.

"I never saw the road..." by Donna Lee from WHAT HAVE YOU LOST?, poems selected by Naomi Shihab Nye. Copyright © 1999 by Donna Lee. Published by HarperCollins Publishers, Inc. All rights reserved.

"The History Teacher" from QUESTIONS ABOUT ANGELS: POEMS by Billy Collins. Copyright © 1991 by Billy Collins. Reprinted by permission of University of Pittsburgh Press. All rights reserved.

"Numbers" by Mary Cornish from POETRY magazine, June 2000. Copyright © 2000 by The Modern Poetry Association. Reprinted by permission of POETRY magazine.

"The Unwritten" by W. S. Merwin from TRUTH & LIES: AN ANTHOLOGY OF POEMS, edited by Patrice Vecchione. Copyright © 1972 by W. S. Merwin. Reprinted by permission of The Wylie Agency, Inc.

# Art Acknowledgments

Cover Illustrations: tl: Melissa Leslie, Nicole/Artwork from The Scholastic Art & Writing Awards/www.artandwriting.org via SODA; tr: Vantino Peaches, Self Portrait/Artwork from The Scholastic Art & Writing Awards/www.artandwriting.org via SODA; bl: Hasan Marius, Untitled/Artwork from The Scholastic Art & Writing Awards/www.artandwriting.org via SODA; br: Anne Lindberg, Self/Artwork from The Scholastic Art & Writing Awards/www.artandwriting.org via SODA; Page 7: Joanna Barnum, Kate in the Mirror/Artwork from The Scholastic Art & Writing Awards; Page 14: Keri & Jarod, Artwork from The Scholastic Art & Writing Awards/www.artandwriting.org via SODA; Page 19: Phoebe Lithgow, Untitled/Artwork from The Scholastic Art & Writing Awards/www.artandwriting.org via SODA; Page 27: Kyung Bae, Self Portrait/Artwork from The Scholastic Art & Writing Awards/www.artandwriting.org via SODA.